My Story:
From Deathbed to Glory

God Still Answers Prayers Today

Brenda Elkins Tricome

My Story: From Deathbed to Glory
Copyright © 2014 by Brenda Tricome

Edited by Erin Roth, Wise Owl Editing

Cover design by: Brenda Tricome

Formatting by Angela McLaurin, Fictional Formats

Table of Contents

Dedication

*I dedicate this book to my God in heaven
for giving me hope, peace and direction for my life.
For never leaving me. And for blessing me beyond measure.*

*To my husband, Tony, for being by my side for 22 years,
for loving me at my worst,
and for encouraging me through my daily struggles.*

To my son, Jared, for motivating me through my darkest hours.

*To my daughter, Jada, for reminding me
of the simple things in life.*

Preface

This book tells about my picture perfect family and how in the blink of an eye, our lives were changed forever. I go through details about my story and God's handiwork throughout my journey. God still performs miracles and answers prayers. God has brought me from my deathbed to glory. We all have a story to tell. It doesn't depend on your age, your race, or your religion. It has nothing to do with your bank account. We all go through trials and tribulations. My purpose for writing this book is out of obedience to God. I strongly felt him urging me and speaking to my heart, telling me to write. I pray that I can inspire you to keep pushing on, to keep getting up when life knocks you down. I pray that I will encourage you to seek out the one and only true God. I pray that it will bring you peace and hope on your journey through life, whether you're seeking spiritual guidance, physical health, financial strain, or help with marriage/relationship issues. My journey has taught me that I can ask for help. I believed in God for years, but now I go to him first, no matter what my problems is. I realized that we don't have to be alone through life's storms and trials; you can get into a relationship with the only one who can change your circumstances.

Prayer works. With hundreds of people praying for me, God healed my body! I know that I am a miracle. The purpose of this book is to tell you that Jesus is alive and he will be coming back for us one day Matthew 24:1-14; 42-44(NIV). Pray and seek God. Read the Bible, it is our instruction book for life. Learn what your purpose is in this life.

A Brief History

I'd like to share some history about myself. I'm the youngest of four kids. I was raised by single mother. She was a great mom. If I had to say one word about how she raised us it would be LOVE. She had so much love for us. We definitely were not the easiest kids to raise, but we never felt unloved.

My father was never in the picture. I would see him once every few years. I grew up energetic and athletic. When I was seven years old, I cut the bottom of my foot, almost off. I stepped on a broken Pepsi bottle. Back then the bottles were glass. I cut the nerves and tendons severely and ended up with 38 stitches across the bottom & side of my foot. I had a long hospital stay and some rehab after that but I was young and persistent to recover. I had to keep up with my siblings. I still have some issues with that foot but I don't let it hinder my activities. I remember getting a letter in the mail from my dad during my recovery. It was one of two letters I had ever gotten. He asked how my foot was doing. I was thrilled to receive it and still have it today.

My mom taught us about God and Jesus at home, but we didn't go to church regularly. I do remember going to a Baptist church when I was young a few times. I didn't like it at all. I was the youngest, so my siblings were all in a class together and I was with kids I didn't know. Needless to say, I was not a fan of church. We were good people, but we didn't practice religion much in our home.

I have always believed in God and even tried to pray from a young age, but I never really understood God or the Bible. I did try and read the Bible some throughout my teenage years, but I had a hard time understanding it. I used to believe if I was good enough, then I would go to heaven, that if I did more good than bad then I was safe. I now know the truth. The book of Ephesians 2:8-9(NIV) "For it is by grace you have been saved, through faith-and not from yourselves, it is the gift of God- not by works, so that no one can boast."

Tony and I met in 1990. We fell in love quickly and just knew we wanted to get married and start a family someday. Tony was a non-practicing Catholic and I was a non-practicing Baptist. What religion would we be? We visited a few local churches but neither of us were happy. It just didn't feel right. Tony received an invitation in the mail, a large, colorful, eye-catching postcard, to learn about Bible facts and events from the Book of Revelation. The classes were held at a Seventh Day Adventist church. First he attended, then both of us. It was interesting; we had never heard anything like it before. We were learning about sin and end-time prophecies. We began making changes in our lives to adapt to what we were being taught. We quickly learned (with the help of our brother-in-law) that much of what we were being taught was not biblically accurate. Our brother-in-law sat with us and explained the Bible. He taught us about the Old Testament (before Christ), and the New Testament (after Christ) and how there that there are 66 books in the Bible.

We were very confused. We just wanted to find a church that practiced the Bible—the whole Bible, nothing added to it and nothing left out or taken out of context. We struggled to find the right religion and the right place for us. From that point on we decided to study the Bible on our own, pray, and ask God what religion he wanted us to be. After months of searching, studying, and praying, God showed us we had to stop searching for a religion and just search for him. Matthew 7:7(NIV) "Ask and it will be given to you; seek and you will find; knock and the door will be opened to you."

In the fall of 1994 we prayed and gave our hearts to the Lord. We committed our relationship and our lives to God. We understood that God was looking for a relationship with us, not a religion. We were married in 1995. That year, Tony suffered from a back injury at work. He was out of work for about a year. We had financial strain to say the least. I worked two jobs and we still struggled to get by. There were times when we didn't know where our next meal would come from, but God has always provided for us.

In 1995, prophets visited our church. According to the Bible, a prophet is a person to whom God gives a special message to be passed on to others. True prophets of God can predict, unlike psychics and false prophets; a biblical prophet will never make an error when it comes to foretelling the future. Why? Because that is God's way of demonstrating that the person really is authorized by God. We had learned about prophets and such during our studying, but this was our first encounter actually seeing one. I confess I was skeptical, but I knew it was biblical.

Deuteronomy18:18 (ESV), "I will raise up a prophet like you from among the brothers."

Hosea 12:10 (NIV), "I spoke to the prophets, gave them many visions and told parables through them."

I opened myself to it. We stood there with many other people and the prophet began praying over us. My eyes were closed. He said a few things over me but what I remember standing out the most to me was him saying he sees me writing something for the Lord. He said he saw writing, writing, writing—a lot of writing going on. I thought, not even close. I laughed and whispered, "Yeah, right!" I wasn't trying to be disrespectful, it's just that this prophecy was so not for me. The prophet said I would be writing something for Lord. Well, I never liked writing, I never had an interest in writing, and I didn't have anything to write about.

Later, when Tony and I talked about the prophetic word, we both thought that it seemed incorrect, unbelievable really. We dismissed it for a while, though every now and then one of us would bring it up and joke about it. This went on for years, and then we both forgot about it. I was positive that writing was not in my future. I wasn't calling God a liar, but I surely didn't have the faith to believe I would ever write anything. Now I know that back in 1995, I didn't have anything of substance to write about. God certainly gave me plenty to write about in the years following. Who knew what my picture perfect family would be facing? God knew!

I was reminded of the prophet's words a year or so into my recovery. I quickly dismissed that word. I chose not to think about it. I think a part of me, deep down in my heart, knew that someday, somehow, it would come to pass, but the idea was hard to accept. God was relentless on this; the feelings grew stronger as the years passed, but I was reluctant and ignored them. Over the course of 14 years, I was told by dozens of people that I should write a book, a testimonial about my life. Still, I felt it wasn't an option for me.

In the summer of 2012, I took a class at my church called Practicing Greatness. I recommend this class to everyone. I learned a lot about myself in those classes— why I am the way I am, what makes me act the way I act. The class taught me to evaluate myself from childhood through adulthood. I grew spiritually, and was able to let go of some baggage I been holding on to for years. I enjoyed the time with all of those special ladies. I shared my testimony for the first time in front of 20 plus people. I had shared it many times before, but with only one or two people at a time. A few of the ladies asked me afterward if I had ever thought about writing a book. I thought, *wow, if I hear this one more time...* I knew that I needed to start praying about writing. I hadn't prayed about it before because I felt if

God showed me through prayer that he wanted me to write, then I would have to be obedient, and I simply did not want to write. Due to migraines, tendonitis in my hands & elbows, memory and concentration issues, I didn't think I could physically do it. I thought writing a book was for extremely educated people, not for ordinary people like me. I thought I had too many deficiencies to write a book. Well, God showed me that I could and would write a book.

Philippians 4:13(NKJV) "I can do all things through Christ who gives me strengthens me."

Part One:
My Story Begins

1998 was one of the best years of my life, but it was also the most challenging year of my life. I was a 26-year-old, happily married woman who just had a healthy baby boy. My husband and I could not be happier. I was young and healthy with a great job that allowed flexibility for my new family. Though our money was tight from time to time, we certainly felt blessed with the most precious son ever born. He was born April 5, 1998, and weighed 6lb 12oz. I remember we paused and prayed in the delivery room, thanking the Lord for him. It felt so unreal, the day of his arrival had finally come. We didn't know what we were having, so still undecided on a boy name, we called him Pumpkin. After nine hours of deliberating, we went with the name Jared Anthony Tricome. Jared was a name suggested by our niece. Jared was the second oldest person who ever lived in the Bible. The book of Genesis says he lived 962 years. We never heard the name before and thought living that long was interesting.

Life was good. Adjusting to our new arrival was great! I remember not getting much sleep, but he could do no wrong. Our lives revolved around this tiny little person. We didn't want to miss anything—expressions, sounds, smiles—everything was perfect and precious. It was hard to leave him to go back to work. I went back part-time at first. Like most new moms, I phoned home often to check on him. We did everything as a family. Life was great.

When Jared was seven months old, he got his first cold. Poor little guy was so sick, he was up all night every night for a good week. We loved on him, prayed over him, and took him to the doctor, but there wasn't much they could do for him at his young age. We were told to just wait it out. As parents, it felt like an eternity to see our baby sick even with just a cold and nothing we could do to fix it.

He got better after a week or so and we were so relieved. I remember washing everything I could and disinfecting the house. I had to do anything I could to prevent another cold, as if it were possible. It's funny now to look back on being new parents—the worrying, the sleepless nights, the inexperience. You really don't know or understand how much love you have in your heart for another human being until you become a parent. Most parents would agree that they would give their right arm for their child. Give their last breath for their child. No sacrifice is too great for our children. That's the love of a parent.

Jared was doing well and thriving, but now Mom wasn't feeling well. Even though I wasn't a regular doctor-goer, I went quickly to see my doctor in hopes to get medicine to prevent of spread whatever I had back to my healthy baby. My symptoms were an awful pain in my head, sore throat, stuffy nose, sometimes runny nose, and my body hurt all over. I hadn't been sick since I was a kid, so this debilitating of a sickness was surprising to me. Looking back, I see that my body was rundown from lack of sleep with Jared being sick the week before and my crazy work life. My boss wanted me to work more hours and I had some employees leave unexpectedly, so I was covering their shifts. I was exhausted. My doctor gave me penicillin. I was thrilled. I thought, *great, this will be over soon.* Well, after five days went by, I was still working and trying to be the Proverbs 31 wife & mom, and let me tell you, it wasn't working. I called my doctor and asked to be seen again. I explained that my head was getting worse and that I felt the medicine wasn't working. They told me to complete my prescription and if I wasn't any better at the end of it, to call back and they would see me.

The pain in my head got worse by the day. I thought I was dying of a tumor. My other symptoms seemed a little better, but the pain in my head was getting to be unbearable! I'd had migraines since I was an adolescent and always had a high tolerance for pain, but it got to the point where I didn't know how much more I could take.

I remember it was a Sunday evening. I was supposed to have a staff meeting at the store where I worked, but my head was splitting. I knew there was no way I could go to the meeting, so I called my shift manager. I asked her to come to my house & pick up the meeting material so she could do the meeting for me. My shift manager hung the phone up on me, so I called right back. I told her who I was and what I wanted. She hung up again. Well, I remember being pretty angry. I yelled for my husband to come upstairs to our room where I was. I explained the phone calls, what she said and what I said, etc. He phoned her and asked her why she hung up on me twice. She told him that she didn't know it was me, that I sounded like an oriental person prank calling her. She apologized. We were confused. I didn't realize my words were so slurred or that my speech had changed so noticeably. I remember it was hard to speak, but I thought it was because of the pain in my head. I remember my eyes were spinning and I couldn't control them or focus. My husband asked me to go to Urgent Care but I declined. I thought, *it's late in the evening, I just needed to sleep and it would be better.* My mom had come over to help take care of Jared while Tony worked and took care of things. I remember I didn't have an appetite. I just took sips of water and stayed in my dark, quiet room. At that point, it had been a day and a half since I really seen my baby. I missed him, but I didn't want him to get sick again. My husband wanted to stay home from volleyball practice that Sunday night. I remember urging him to go. He had been doing many of my chores and baby duties all week and I thought he could use a break, besides, my mom was there taking care of Jared and myself if I needed anything. My mother-in-law also stopped by to check on me. She noticed my speech was very slurred. Both moms thought I should go to the Emergency room, I said no. I stayed in bed for a couple more hours and I prayed. I asked God to stop the pain and what I should do. My pain was getting worse and worse.

I got up and went down the stairs, which seemed to take me forever. I was very dizzy and could hardly walk, but I made it to the couch. I knew my husband would be home any minute from practice. When he got home it was around 10:30 pm, and I told him I was ready to go to Urgent Care. I needed to hold Tony's arm walking into Urgent Care because I couldn't focus my eyes and felt extremely dizzy. I told the first person at the desk why I was there and what my symptoms were. I told the second person the same thing, and then the doctor. I tried to tell him with the help of Tony, but they just weren't understanding either of us! I kind of yelled at them and said, "I don't talk like this, I don't walk like this."

They looked at Tony and said, "Oh, your wife doesn't normally speak like this?"

Tony was frustrated—that's what we'd been trying to tell them this whole time!

Then they rushed me to the hospital by ambulance. Every bump in the road, every sound I heard, was killing my head. I remember vomiting in the ambulance and thinking, *I just can't take this pain anymore.* I thought we would never get there. I could see Tony following behind me in our car. Finally, we arrived at the emergency room. As we got checked in, I remember being annoyed and frustrated that I had to repeat my symptoms all over again and my pain had gotten worse. I felt like I was dying! Quickly they gave me an I.V. of morphine for the pain; the relief was wonderful. That was the best I'd felt in over a week. Not long after my relief, the pain came back just as badly. I told them I needed more morphine many times. They gave me some more, but it wasn't helping me. Nothing was helping this pain! The Emergency Room was so loud and so bright—simply unbearable for me.

Finally, they told us they had a room for me. Inside, I was smiling ear to ear, because I knew I was getting out of the ER and away from the noise and the lights into a quiet room. I praised God in my head and couldn't get to my room fast enough. A sweet little old lady lay next to me, my new roommate. We were separated by a curtain. I was sad to find out that this lady was dying. She had lots of company, in fact, she was having a party. Family members were there, coming back and forth with food, reminiscing, yelling, laughing etc.

I totally felt like I was dying from the pain in my head. I rang the nurse bell. No one came. I started thinking things in my mind, unkind things like I wished these people would leave and just turn off the lights— *Hello, I'm dying over here, please just give me some relief!* I felt like

I was being selfish because I just wanted them all to go! I remember asking God to forgive me for being so selfish. I prayed for that old lady and her family. What a blessing for her to have all of her loved ones around one last time sharing a meal. I knew I was being selfish, but I couldn't take the pain anymore. I was in tears. I reached for a Kleenex but my hand wouldn't do it. I couldn't grip and pull the Kleenex out. In frustration, I hit the Kleenex box, knocking it to the floor, thinking, *oh God, what is wrong with me?*

My husband was out talking to doctors and nurses and trying to get me into a private room. I got up to go to the bathroom, which was just a few steps away, but still in my room. I got up and slowly started walking, but suddenly realized that I couldn't walk well enough, not even for those few steps, so I grabbed the wall and kind of leaned on it, hugging it until I got in the bathroom, barely realizing that I was mooning the party next to me, as I needed both hands to hold the wall. Honestly, I couldn't have cared less at that point! Many hours had gone by since I was in the ER and the doctors still didn't know what was wrong with me. All we knew was the pain was unbearable and now I couldn't control my hands, walk well, or talk normally.

My first miracle happened when a good friend of ours, who happened to be a nurse at the hospital, was able to switch patients around on her floor to get me into a private, dark, quiet room. I couldn't begin to express my gratitude for that. I could never repay her! That was one of the most helpful things for me at that point. It brings tears to my eyes just thinking about it and how much it helped me—how it helped my head!

I don't remember much after moving into the private room. My husband tells me I had 3 spinal taps done. I do remember the taps because they held me forward and apologized for how much they were going to hurt. I told the doctors that I didn't feel any pain other than what was going on in my head. After many tests, doctors confirmed I had viral meningitis. They said if you're going to have meningitis, viral is the one you want because bacterial meningitis is deadly. Apparently with viral meningitis, you're usually sick a week or so and it's over.

I thought, *yeah, great, but then why am I not over it?* I was confused. I had been sick for week at home already. It seemed like my pain was worsening by the hour. Other things were worse too. I got to the point that when I spoke, no one understood me. I couldn't touch my nose when they asked me to. I couldn't say my name or answer questions. I tried to say "Tony" and "Jared" the best I could, but they couldn't understand me. I still knew what was going on in my mind, but was confused as to why I couldn't verbalize my thoughts or control my hands.

My poor husband was by my side every minute. My mom was at our home taking care of Jared. I remember talking to my mom on the phone when I first arrived and settled in the ER, after my first dose of morphine. I struggled to talk, but I asked her to take care of Jared for me and not to leave him with anyone. I had no idea what was wrong with me. I worried about Jared with both Daddy and I gone all night and now into the next day, but I knew he was in good hands. I was an over-protective mom then and I still am. She let me talk to Jared. I kept thinking about how he held the phone and me getting to listen to his every sound, reveling in the sound of his breathing. He was so sweet. This was the longest I had been away from him. My symptoms came on so fast, so strong, at home that my mom kept Jared downstairs and I stayed away from him upstairs. I could remember that and how much I missed him. I thought, *God, what is wrong with me? I just want*

to go home and be a wife and a mom and have things back to normal!

Unfortunately, I got worse. It had been few days to a week in my private room. The doctors didn't know why I wasn't getting over this, so I was sent to the Intensive Care Unit. I remember parts of being in the ICU, but I was told that I was in and out of it a lot. I was confused. I couldn't understand any of this. I knew that I was sick for longer than a week, so if it's viral meningitis, why was I still sick? Why was my head still hurting so badly? I remember sometimes opening my eyes and seeing different family members and friends, which was confusing and very frustrating, because I couldn't communicate to them. I felt so awkward just lying there. Sometimes I'd wake up to people trying to push food on me or to get me to drink. It was so strange! I definitely had no appetite, no thought of food. I just wanted to sleep. I was exhausted. Opening my eyes felt like work; that alone wore me out. One time I heard talking and opened my eyes to see the doctor talking with Tony. He told him to prepare himself and that if I survived through the night, he likely wouldn't recognize me. He told my husband that I wouldn't be the Brenda he knew. He said something about me being in a vegetative state. Well, I understood everything I'd just heard, so that blew my mind. I thought, *wow, I'm really that bad? That sick?*

I was still in and out of it. I really couldn't communicate my thoughts or indicate that I understood the doctor. The next time I opened my eyes, I saw Tony, who said a good friend of ours came to see me and to check on us, and that he and his wife have been praying for me, like many others. He ended up staying all night with Tony in the waiting room at that very critical time. We will always be grateful to him and his wife.

We were told that I was on many prayer chains and prayer lists. At least three different churches were praying for me. People in other states were praying for me (they didn't even know me). Another friend of ours worked at a local warehouse and would get a few guys together and meet in the men's room to pray for me every morning. I know, right? Who does that? I thought the same thing.

Another time, I opened my eyes and looked around to see my pastor, the late Paul Wagner. He was with the elders of the church, right there in the ICU, praying over me and anointing my head with oil.

James 5:14 (NKJV), "Is anyone among you sick? Let him call for the elders of the church, and let them pray over him, anointing him with oil in the name of the Lord."

I could not believe my eyes. I know this is very biblical, but I thought, *wow, Pastor Paul is here to see me.* I thought I must be very sick and the nurses were going to think we're some radical Christians. I remember grinning inside and looking around at everyone that was there at that time. There were nurses crying; I'm sure they had never seen anything like this before. It really was amazing! The spirit of God was definitely in that ICU room! I'll never forget looking into Pastor Paul's eyes and him telling me to get better and that they were there for us no matter what we needed. I just cried and tried to mumble my thanks to him as he hugged me goodbye. Then Tony told me that he would walk them out and would be right back. I remember fighting to keep my eyes open. I wanted to say goodnight to Tony, but I was so tired. I kept peeking to see if he was back yet.

I started to pray, realizing I must be pretty sick if Pastor Paul came all the way up here to see me.

I prayed to God in my mind:

Lord, I guess I'm that sick. You know my favorite song is "It is Well with My Soul." Well, Lord, take me home. If you want to bring me home now, then I'm okay with that. Lord, I want whatever your will is, that's what I want. So take me home.

My eyes were extremely heavy. I opened them again

to see if Tony was back, and as I felt my eyes closing, I had the realization that I had a baby. I remember saying, "Hey, wait a minute, God, I have a baby! Lord, I prayed for almost a year to get pregnant and I promised you that I would train that baby in all of your ways, so I need to go home and do that, Lord. You need to heal me, Lord, and make me well again. Yes, I totally reneged on my first prayer."

I must have fallen asleep. I don't know how long I was asleep, but I was awakened by a doctor, one that I didn't recognize. He said he needed to do surgery on me, that he had to drill a small hole in and make a small incision in my head. I had fluid and swelling of the brain called cerebellitis. The doctor wanted to put a shunt in to drain my brain. I freaked out and called for Tony, but he didn't understand me. My nurse ran over to me; she knew I was scared and understood that I wanted my husband. She explained that to the doctor and that I wanted him to call Tony. I kept yelling and pointed to the phone on the wall, freaking out because I didn't know if this was really what I needed. I had no idea what day it was or what was wrong with me. I was totally dependent on Tony. I certainly couldn't speak for myself.

So he called Tony. I heard him explain what he was

going to do and he told Tony he didn't need to be there for this, that he had to do this procedure now or I may not live. I'm told that I didn't wake up much for a couple of days. When I did open my eyes, I immediately looked around for Tony. He was my rock through all of this. He was the only familiar thing in my life for weeks and by my side every day. He only went home to shower and see Jared then came right back to me.

I was somewhat with it in my mind when I woke up. I knew I had a baby and I knew who my visitors were, but I was confused about what happened to me and what was going on around me. I didn't know the day or how many days had passed. What I did know was that the awful pain in my head was gone. Praise God! I was uncomfortable, but it was great compared to the pain I'd felt the last time I was awake.

I looked for Tony, but I saw my mom and my friend; Tony had gone home to see Jared and to give mom a break so she could visit me. When I opened my eyes, I saw them and said, "Angels! Angels!" At this point I hadn't spoken in weeks, other than struggling to say "Tony" or "baby," and it was hardly understandable. I think I was shouting it because I was excited; I don't think I could express much emotion on my face, but I was super excited and I wanted to scream it to the rooftops. At this point I wasn't concerned with my health. I just want to share my awesome angelic experience.

My friend came closer to me and put her ear to my lips, so I quickly figured out I wasn't shouting. I was confused, but not about what I saw. I had seen beautiful angels. I heard the most beautiful music, nothing seen or heard in this world! Nothing like you would imagine. Nothing that Hollywood could create. It was from heaven and I wanted to shout it out for all to hear!

However, I could barely whisper it and make it understandable. My friend seemed a little freaked out once she understood me, she asked, "Bren, is it the angel of death coming?" I shook my head no. I thought, *you're crazy, girl*, because I was excited. I felt peace. I knew I was going to be okay! My friend went to tell the nurse that I woke up and what I said.

They rushed in and one of the nurses says, "Oh, honey, she's highly medicated, it's the drugs talking." She went on to explain how people say this or that and they think they see things when BLAH BLAH BLAH.

Well, I tell you, the spirit of slap came over me, but I certainly couldn't reach her nor control my arms or hands to do it, so I just kept shaking my head no. I was so mad inside because I knew what I had seen and what I heard. I knew that God showed me I was going to be okay! My friend knew that something else had happened to me, and it had nothing to do with all the drugs I was on and it wasn't the angel of death coming for me.

The horrible pain in my head was gone. It was a miracle not to feel that pain anymore. I was still extremely tired and out of it for periods of time, though. I woke many times to see different people visiting; my mom, mother-in-law, my sister, friends, cousins, and aunt were all there at one point or another. It was so strange, I would just lie there and they would talk to me, but I couldn't communicate back. I still couldn't control my arms. It seemed many times that I opened my eyes and someone tried to make me drink or offer me food, but that was the last thing on my mind. Once, I awoke to see family from out of town. I thought, *what are you doing here?* I was confused. Apparently when I was at my worst, my family was called in. One time I opened my eyes and I had this crazy itch on my head, completely unaware that the top part of my head was shaved, or of the surgery that took place, or that the shunt was in. I guess the dried blood made it itch like crazy, so naturally, I tried to itch it. I was unsuccessful as I couldn't control my hands, and any time

I got close to my head, someone would yell at me to stop so I wouldn't hurt the incision. I didn't remember the surgery at that point—I just wanted to scratch my itch. At that time, my sister came over to me and ever so gently scratched my dirty, dried bloody head repeatedly. Now that's love—I'm just saying.

The constant pushing me to drink and to eat something got old fast. Tony forced me to drink Ensure shakes, which I hated. I yelled at him, and even though none of it was understandable, he knew I was yelling at him. In my mind, he was being mean, forcing me to drink this nasty stuff. I didn't want food or a drink or anything. I didn't realize Tony had been pulled aside and told that if didn't start drinking the Ensure shakes that they would have to put a feeding tube down my throat. He was told that my brain wouldn't recover if I didn't start to drink and eat. It had been a while since I ate or drank anything, but I definitely didn't want a tube in my throat, so I drank those nasty shakes.

Prayer chains were still going on for me from several different churches. The guys at the warehouse were still meeting in the men's room and praying for me every morning. My family and friends and employees were praying for me. So many people were praying. I had never heard of such a thing before. The prayer was so powerful. So many thoughtful, kind people.

I started recovering and getting stronger. I was told that I had brain damage. I had to learn to walk and talk and to control my body all over again. I lost the strength in my hands. I was down for 4-5 weeks at this point. I knew I had a long road ahead of me, but I was definitely getting better. Doctors made me sit up in bed for only minutes at a time at first, then longer durations. I remember crying about it, as it physically hurt to move in to that position. I was frustrated that they had to put me into the sitting position, that I couldn't do it myself. My poor husband did everything they told him to do to help me get better and I fought him on most of it. I realize that now and truly feel bad. I just didn't understand how making me so uncomfortable would help (I'm sorry, Tony). Tony prayed over me and read the Bible to me when I was out of it and at my worst. I may not remember it all, but it was comforting to know. His strong faith during that time was a blessing for both of us.

The big day came sooner than I expected, the day I was going to stand up—with help, of course. I certainly don't remember the exact time, or the exact number of days I was in each room and ICU, but I'm told the time I started to stand was around the sixth week. Tony and I have gone over these weeks numerous times to be as accurate as possible. This was an emotional, exhausting time for Tony as well as myself. They scooted me to the side of the bed, a person on either side of me, and they pulled me up. I felt so wobbly and scared and extremely frustrated that I couldn't do these things on my own. I wondered if I'd ever be able to. It didn't look that way. When we were told that I wouldn't be able to walk alone or function for myself, well, my mind started to reject that and I refused to believe it! We continued these grueling exercises a couple times a day, sitting longer, standing longer, etc. It felt like I had been doing these forever, but I felt myself getting stronger. I thought about my baby constantly. I held his little picture that Tony brought me and looked at it often. I missed him so very, very much. I missed holding and loving on him. I missed his smell and every sound he made. All I could think was I had to get out of there and go home to him. I hadn't seen him since the night I went to Urgent Care. I was so sick, he couldn't be around me, or in the ICU.

Tony called home a couple times over the weeks and set the phone on my ear. Mom held it up to Jared so I could listen to him baby talk and breathe. I just cried; I missed him so much. I knew he had changed so much and I missed it. I felt like he thought his momma abandoned him. My heart broke, but this also gave me new strength to fight harder to go home to him. I prayed and thanked God for my progress every step of the way, and many were baby steps!

Before I knew it, I was walking around the nurses' station with people on both sides of me, thrilled, exhausted, and frustrated all at the same time. Looking into Tony's eyes and knowing how proud he was of me definitely helped, but it's so hard to want to do more, to go another step, when it's physically impossible.

I believe I'm a strong person and I know God showed me through the angels that I was going to be all right, able, and capable of raising and training my son, so I held on to that and pushed through, past my limit. Every day was a struggle. It felt like I was gone a year, but it had only been six and a half weeks. I could remember some things from the past few weeks, but I was confused with a good amount, also. Some things I was positive about, for example, I knew that I had seen beautiful angels and heard the most angelic music. I was told I had short term memory loss, but I could remembered most everything from years ago.

It amazes me how the human brain works, and how our bodies are made to recover! No one ever believed I'd make it this far. Praise God. In a week's time I was sitting up, standing with help, and walking with help.

Doctors told me that I was ready to move to the rehabilitation center that was connected to Crouse Hospital. I was super excited with my improvements, and getting a little closer to going home. The facility seemed nice and very clean. Everyone was friendly and positive. I was in the unit with the stroke victims and people with brain injuries. It was sad to see so many people like me and worse. As I looked around I saw people of all ages struggling to walk, talk, and to feed themselves. The staff encouraged all of us to try and do daily tasks like getting dressed, brushing teeth, and feeding ourselves without help, as that was the goal, to get us ready to eventually go home. I worked on strength training, balance, cognitive skills, speech, and memory as well. I could read, but blocks of words on the page jumped. To me, it looked like someone was shaking the paper, but it was really my eyes. I was told that I probably wouldn't be able to drive because of brain damage and memory loss. Doctors were concerned with whether or not I could remember driving rules or respond quickly. I was devastated after that was said, but I chose not to believe it. I couldn't imagine not driving. I just believed that I would continue to get better!

Therapy started right away, all day long, with breaks for breakfast, lunch, dinner.

It was humiliating to see myself try to hit a balloon with a stick as part of my therapy. It sounds easy, but I looked like a small child learning to stand up alone for the first time. I tried my hardest, it just seemed overwhelming for me to think of standing up alone, holding on to a stick and actually swinging it all at the same time. I struggled to accept this challenge. I should have been able to do it, and it killed me to admit that I couldn't. I don't know if I ever hit that balloon.

God was definitely working on my pride. I literally would scoot out of my bed and crawl on the floor to the bathroom rather than ask a nurse to help me walk there. I couldn't walk alone yet, I was still too wobbly, so crawling was my only option. I tired myself out crawling, but I was proud that I was able to pull myself up to the toilet and actually go, then instantly deflated because I couldn't grip and pull the toilet paper off the roll. I couldn't control my hands enough to get toilet paper and wipe. I hated the fact that I knew what to do but my brain just wouldn't let me do it. This was probably one of the most frustrating times for me. Still today, anytime I use a public bathroom and the toilet paper gets stuck or it's hard to roll, I flash back to this time.

My husband often showed up at just the right moment, and he or a nurse would find me and help me. They would also help me put my hands together to wash them. I don't know any husbands that would wipe their wives and do the million other things he did.

I can't thank Tony enough for always being there for me. He made a name for himself at the rehab center— Nurse Tony is what they all called him, because he did so much for me. He helped me in the bathroom and when I could finally shower, he washed my hair and body. Being a hairdresser, I must say I could not wait to have my hair washed! He only did the back, as I still had stitches on the top, but it felt great! He also clipped my nails and shaved my legs. He would stand behind me and hold my hand and arm to guide the toothbrush to my mouth and helped me go through the motions of brushing my teeth, like I was a child just learning the skill. He helped get me dressed most days. I know, ladies, he's a keeper, right?

Tony is the greatest man I know. I can't fully express my gratitude and appreciation for him.

As grateful as I was, I was also extremely frustrated

that I couldn't do these daily tasks myself. I felt my pride being stripped away and learned a lot about humility. I worked hard and started gaining strength. Every small achievement pushed me to do more. I couldn't wait for the day that I could do these tasks on my own. I practiced all of my therapy for hours at night in my room. When I was strong enough and could stand alone, I practiced walking heel to toe back and forth across my room. I would lift water bottles up and down several times to get stronger. I practiced reading, writing, counting, and reciting the alphabet. I had a weird twitch in my right thumb that I couldn't control and I wondered if I'd be able to cut hair again. I struggled to feed myself. I often thought about all the things I no longer could do myself. It definitely made me sad, but it also made me determined and excited for my small victories. I consciously would remind myself of things I did that maybe I couldn't have done days prior.

I wanted to be independent.

I didn't like asking for help. I was young and wanted to be independent.

I remember picking up a waffle and eating it like it was a piece of bread because it was such a hassle for me to hold a fork and knife and to cut it. I knew what to do, but my brain didn't let my hands do it. It's embarrassing to admit that there was more than one occasion when I used my sheet as a napkin because opening up the silverware and napkin was too difficult.

People were still praying for me. I could feel the prayers; I was improving every day. People sent me cards, flowers, and many friends dropped off groceries at our house and things for Jared. The response was unbelievable. Many of the people we didn't even know. I also received cards and little messages of hope. Little angel keepsakes were brought to the hospital and the rehab center, some from strangers. I know God hears our prayers.

I thank everyone who has prayed for me and my family, and for the cards and keepsakes, etc. All of your time and efforts were a huge encouragement to me. Today, I still keep one of the angels and a couple of the messages of hope on my dresser. I will always cherish them.

Back in therapy, I had to carry a large, weighted ball around the gym floor. They told me to pretend it was my baby so I could gain the strength to carry him. I worked hard and practiced everything they told me to. I was so eager to go home. I missed Jared so much.

Finally, after seven weeks or so of not seeing my

baby, I got a visit from my mom and my precious little baby. He was eight and a half months old. They walked into my rehab room and the first thing Jared did was point to me and say, "Momma." I started to cry. They brought him right to me and set him in my arms. I held him so tight. That moment was one of the best moments of my life. I thought, *how does he know I'm his momma? He hasn't seen me in almost two months.* The top of my head was shaved and I was huge from steroids. I could hardly talk to where I was understandable.

My mom shared with us that every day she would hold Jared up and point to a picture of Tony and me on our living room wall and she would say, "Momma." She did this every day, several times a day, so when he saw me, he'd know I was his momma. It was the best feeling of my life.

He had changed so much. He had much more hair and new teeth. He could say "Momma" as clear as a bell. Unfortunately, I didn't have the strength to hold the wiggly guy, but I had a great visit with him, my mom, and Tony. It broke my heart when our visit ended. I didn't want them to leave. I cried when they left. I was so sad. I think I cried every day after that because I missed him and wanted to go home to him.

I got really good at holding Jared's picture up and showing it to all the doctors and nurses. I used to sleep with it at night. Every time a doctor or therapist came in to talk to me, I would extend it out to them, almost forcing them to look at my baby. I would cry and show them his picture, hoping they would understand how much I missed him and needed to go home. But what happened was they sent in a psychologist to question me; they thought I was depressed. The psychologist recommended some depression medication and asked me if I wanted to try it. I couldn't speak clearly, but I tried to get her to understand that she should ask Tony about that. She made it clear that I could decide for myself and we did not need to ask Tony. She said it was my decision. I hadn't made a decision about anything in almost two months, especially concerning my health. I thought that was a good sign if she thought I was well enough to decide for myself. I expressed to her the best way I knew how that I was not depressed, I just missed my baby. I did *not* want any medications. I continued working hard with all of my therapy. In my room at night, I worked on everything they asked me to do.

Like all new parents, we were looking forward to Jared's first Christmas. I certainly never ever thought something like this would happen. I knew the gifts I wanted to buy for him and anticipated him trying to open his presents. It made me sad to think I would miss my baby's first Christmas. I prayed and asked God not to let me miss it. I prayed that we would all be together. Tony and I asked all the doctors if I would be home for Christmas. I tried to convince them that I was fine and ready, but they said no. I didn't give up; I kept asking and explaining that it was my baby's first Christmas—I *had* to be home for it.

I was walking by myself just after the second or third day in rehab, slow and kind of steady, but I was doing it and I was cleared to walk by myself. I was much stronger, and slowly improving my speech…slowly improving my everything. I pleaded my case again, this time begging them to let me go home for Christmas, even for just a few hours. I said I promised I would come right back, but please don't let me miss my baby's Christmas.

Well, a miracle happened. They told us that I could go home on Christmas Day under Tony's supervision, that I could leave the rehab center for four hours if Tony promised to bring me right back. We were overwhelmed with joy. Ecstatic!

On Christmas morning, I woke up early and got

myself dressed and ready (it took a long time, but I did it myself) for Tony to pick me up. I was very self-conscious about my appearance and the way I walked and talked. I worried what people were going to think of me, but really, I just wanted to be home with my family. I was so very thankful for that day.

Tony arrived right on time to pick me up. The doctor gave him a list of instructions for me— basically I could sit and visit my family and that was it. I was ecstatic to be going home. I held Tony's arm as he helped me walk safely outside. The fresh air was great. I still had the IV needle in my arm. Both of my arms were bruised from shots and IVs. My belly was covered in bruises from six plus weeks of daily injections to prevent blood clots. I really think I was in shock that they allowed me to leave for four hours, but I was afraid to share any of that because I thought maybe they would change their mind. I guess they trusted Tony. He practically lived there with me, so they got to know him pretty well. And I'm sure I was pretty pathetic with my crying and asking to go home all the time. God gave them favor for me.

It felt so good to be out of there. Tony asked me a dozen times if I was okay throughout my visit, he was so attentive and caring. My reply was the same every time—

"I'm fine!" The truth is, everything seemed to be moving in high speed. Everything but me. My brain was definitely in overload. Christmas 1998 was definitely a memorable one to say the least, but I was alive and I got to go home for a little while to be with my family and to celebrate our Lord's birth! This was a special day. Once I got home, Tony helped me plop into the recliner, where I stayed until it was time to return to rehab. My mom brought Jared right over to me and sat him on my lap. I remember how good he smelled, fresh out of the bath. His hair was so soft and there was so much more of it. He had changed his looks and was so big. I remember thinking, *wow, he's so active, so heavy.* I hardly had the strength to hold him or pick him up even with help. I kept thanking God for letting me be home for his first Christmas. I celebrated Christmas with Tony, Jared, my mom, and my sister. I enjoyed watching every move Jared made. His growth and development was intriguing to me. He maneuvered around so fast now. He attempted to open his presents. My sister helped him open his gifts, then she and Tony put his toys together for him. He played with some things; he loved his new Cookie Monster that laughed when you squeezed its tummy. I enjoyed watching him play with the bows and wrapping paper too.

Inside, I was feeling overwhelmed. This was a lot of commotion for me. I opened a couple of gifts from my mom; it made her happy. I tried to keep a smile on my face and a grateful heart. Everything was challenging and wore me out, but I did it. I only spoke if I had to, responding with one-word answers or a nod of the head. I can honestly say that these were the most overwhelming four hours of my life. Part of me was overwhelmed with the joy of being home with my family, seeing my baby on his first Christmas, and the other part was just plain overwhelmed and I couldn't wait to go back to my room at the rehabilitation center and lay down, though I would've never admitted that then.

My sister bought me a beautiful 2 ½ foot angel that lit up for Christmas. I cried as she was so beautiful and the meaning went straight to my heart because of the angels I saw while I was in the ICU. My sister didn't know that I had seen them or that I heard the most amazing music, she said she saw the angel and she thought of me. It was one of the best gifts I had ever received, at just the right time.

I tried to cuddle and feed Jared his bottle before I had to leave to go back to rehab. Tony set him on my lap with pillows under my arm. I'm so excited to feed him but he was just too heavy for me, and my arms were so sore from needles and bruising. It hurt every time he leaned on the needle in my arm, but I was so thrilled to be with him and hold him that I couldn't think of that. I struggled to hold him and he wiggled down to the floor, looking for his grandma, so I ask her to take him. I was a little sad, but I understood that they'd gotten close.

When we returned to my room at rehab, I felt a sigh of relief as I laid down on my bed. I was exhausted! I was blown away that I made it four hours. I never moved, I just laid there, praying, until I fell asleep. I couldn't thank God enough for the best Christmas present—going home for my baby's first Christmas.

As I slept, I awoke to a young girl crying out for her mom. She'd lost her family in a house fire. I was told she had brain damage from the smoke. She cried for her mommy every night and called out for her. I remember praying for her and many other people that I became acquainted with in the rehab facility. I had conflicting emotions about the entire place; I felt guilty that I was recovering so quickly and these people had been here for several months or longer, but I was so proud of my hard work and results. It just wasn't fair. Believe me, I wanted to have a full quick recovery, I wanted out of there for good, but my heart broke for her and others that weren't getting better.

I asked God, *Why? Why am I improving so fast and they aren't?* I felt so confused, but thankful at the same time. All I could do is pray for them.

My therapy was going well. My least favorite was speech therapy. I found it very humiliating. The therapist recorded me reading a baby book and then played it back for Tony and me. She said I needed to bring my voice up and down and pointed out how monotone I sound. She said I needed to learn to speak with expression in my voice. If only she could've heard the expressions in my head! I was so very embarrassed. That was my least favorite part of therapy. I just hated talking at all. I did want to be able to read books to my baby, though. That thought pushed me to try and do everything she said. Progress was slower in this area, but it was progress.

Seven days and seven nights, one long week, passed. I was told that I was improving leaps and bounds, more than they ever anticipated. They said if I had 24-hour care at home, then I could go home and continue my therapy doing outpatient care 3-4 days a week for the next 6-8 weeks, and then follow up with CT scans and doctor appointments.

Tony had to return to work; he hadn't worked since I first got sick in November. My mom agreed to move in, which was a huge blessing. She had pretty much moved in already, she'd been at my house taking care of my baby since the whole thing started, but she would move in for real now. I could never repay her. She gave up her life to take care of my baby for almost two months, and then she agreed to move in until I completed all of my therapies and got the okay to be alone.

There's nothing like a mother's love for her child, other than the love of Christ.

I was so excited to be going home. I couldn't wait to feel normal again. I was told that I had the shortest stay at the rehabilitation center in the history of the facility being open. No one had ever stayed such a short time and recovered as fast as I had. All I could say was, "Praise God" and thank everyone for all of the prayers. I was excited with the thought of holding my baby, and rocking him, and seeing him every day. I looked forward to seeing him reach all his milestones and to be a real family again.

Part Two:
Rejection and God's voice

It was so great being home. It felt like I had been gone so long. It had been about seven and a half weeks. At home, things were certainly harder than I expected; there were definitely more obstacles than at the rehab center.

It's an awful feeling to not be able to cook for your family or give your own baby a bath. It broke my heart that I still couldn't carry my baby or pick him up by myself. My mom would sit him on my lap with pillows supporting my arms so I could hold him and try to feed him. This was great, and very enjoyable for a couple of minutes, but then he would try and squirm himself down. I just couldn't hold on to him or control him. He had gotten *very* attached to his grandma and wanted her all the time. He pointed to her and tried to climb down off my lap every time I tried to feed him or hold him. So I told her to take him and she could feed him; I got upset and frustrated and went upstairs.

I felt rejected. This had happened pretty much every day for several weeks. One night, I had reached my breaking point. I remember telling her to just take him and she could rock him to sleep. I was so upset I tried to storm up the stairs, but I was still struggling on the stairs. I made it up to his room and sat on his bedroom floor in the dark, just me and God. I was crying, more like sobbing, so hurt and angry that my son didn't want me anymore! I started talking to God.

"Why, God? Why? After everything I've been through and everything I'm still going through, I've have never questioned you, never asked why this all happened to me. But my heart is broken, Lord! I fought so hard to come home to take care of my baby! It was him who kept me going and kept me pushing harder. Then I come home and he doesn't want me at all! He wants his grandma!"

I continued crying out to God, sobbing with anger and frustration.

"Why, God, why?" I said again. "I've never questioned my sickness, but why this, the one thing I fought so hard for?"

A clear voice said, "Now you know how I feel."

I was a little spooked and looked behind me, knowing I was the only one there in Jared's dark room, but I definitely heard this audible voice, so I said, "What? I don't understand," and God showed me in that moment that is exactly how he feels—rejected.

This is exactly what he wants from us; you and me. From all of his children. God wants us to want him. He wants to be wanted. He wants us to go to him first, not to a friend or spouse or boyfriend /girlfriend. He wants us to bring our problems to him. He just wants us to want him, like I wanted Jared to want me!

I cried and told God I was sorry and that I got it now. I understood loud and clear!

I have never been the same since that night. God has changed me and my perspective. I now look at people through God's eyes and I look at every situation in my life through God's eyes.

I got sick in November 1998. I came home January 1, 1999. My life changed 100% during that time.

One of the most amazing things happened next. Tony, Jared and I were visiting friends, one of my first outings post sickness. She was my nurse friend from the hospital, the one that got me the private room. We had a nice visit at her house, sitting around and admiring our kids. We ate a nice meal together and I was actually feeling very relaxed, which was hard for me at that time. My girlfriend says, "Bren, tell me about the angels that you saw while you were in the hospital."

Well, inside I thought, *Oh no, Lord, I can't—please don't make me talk.* This story was so in depth and honestly, I hated talking. Back then, I usually responded with one or two word answers and a lot of nodding because my speech was hard to understand. It was a lot of work trying to process words in my head and get them to come out correctly.

I was embarrassed to talk, but at the same time I felt that I owed her. I was so grateful to her and her family. It was so important to me when she got me that dark, quiet room when (at that time) I literally felt like my life depended on it. So I quietly asked God to help me speak clearly and I shared what happened to me while I was in the intensive care. I explained how Pastor Paul and the elders prayed over me and anointed me with oil. I shared my thoughts, my favorite song, "It is Well with My Soul." I told her that I thought, *wow, I guess I'm that sick, Lord, okay, then bring me home, Lord.* I told her about my prayer and that I wanted the Lord's will and I was okay with it, meaning I was ready to go to heaven. I told her about how sleepy I was and that could hardly keep my eyes open. I shared how I then opened my eyes to look for Tony and remembered that I had a baby; that I prayed and said, "Wait a minute, Lord, I have a baby! I prayed a year for him and you gave him to me and I promised you that I would train him in all of your ways, so, Lord, you have to heal my body so I can go home and train him in all of your ways." I admitted to her and God that I reneged on my first prayer.

At this point, I was crying and could hardly speak. Talking about my experience was very emotional for me, especially in the early years, but I continued on, telling her how I was extremely tired and fell asleep and I didn't wake up for a day or two (I only know that because that's what I was told), but when I woke, I saw beautiful angels and heard amazing music. I told her it was like nothing of this world. I said I knew I was going to be okay and explained the incredible peace I felt. I told her the first word I said when I opened my eyes was "angels" and how I had not said anything but "Tony" or "baby" for many weeks prior to that.

Looking back on this now, it is intriguing to me that I felt such a peace and just knew I was going to be okay, because at that time I was still very sick. I couldn't touch my nose when they asked me to and I couldn't talk well. When I saw the angels and heard the music, it gave me peace. I knew I was going to be all right.

I was still crying while sharing my experience with my friend, who was crying too.

She said, "Bren, you don't understand."

I was confused. "No," I responded, "I guess not." I was puzzled. "Understand what?"

"After Pastor Paul and the elders left the ICU from praying over you, they went to church. It was a church night. Pastor Paul stood at the pulpit and asked the congregation to stand up and hold hands across the aisles. He said he had a prayer request and he prayed, 'Lord we pray for Brenda Tricome. We ask that you place an angel in the corner of her hospital room. We pray for her to be healed and to be able to go home and raise and train her baby in all of your ways.'"

Wow, I was blown away by that! There was no way that Tony or I could have known this happened at church. We hadn't been to church since prior to me getting sick. I didn't know what to say except "Praise God."

I thought, *this is amazing. Now I know I'm not crazy, and I definitely didn't make this experience up.* I know what I saw and I know what I heard, and it wasn't the drugs talking! It was my Lord blessing me, showing me angels and letting me hear amazing music, showing me that he was in control. I knew that I had experienced a taste of heaven and that I was going to be okay. My pastor's prayer from the pulpit and my prayer from the Intensive Care Unit were almost the same exact wording—this was a miracle. This was my confirmation of what I had seen and heard.

I truly understand that God healed my body. I was on my deathbed when my husband was told to prepare himself, that I'd never be the same if I survived through the night. Then by chance, a doctor, not even one of my doctors, walked through the ICU unit and noticed something on my monitor and immediately took me in for surgery to put a shunt in my head. Still, we were told of all the things that I wouldn't be able to do again. Well, God certainly proved the doctors wrong. Coincidence? I think not!

It wasn't long after that visit at our friends' house that we attended our regular Saturday church service. It was my first time back in church since getting sick. I was excited to worship and praise God and thank him for all that he has been doing in my life. I was humbled by the love and support from our church family. As I walked into church, many people, some of whom were strangers, surrounded me. Many hugged me and said how blessed they were to see me, and that they had been praying for me. I didn't know some of the people; I recognized them from church, maybe said hi or gave them a smile or a nod over the years, but we weren't acquainted. I was humbled by the outpouring of genuine love and concern for me. My husband and I both were amazed and humbled. Anyone can go to a church, but to belong and to be a part of such a large family is amazing. It's overwhelming. We could never say thank you enough for all of the love, prayers and support that I received from Believers Chapel.

I was feeling pretty shaky from so many people coming up to me as we walked in. Back then, I lost my balance if I got nervous or had a lot of commotion around me. We made it into the sanctuary. I was relieved and just want to focus on God and thank him for healing me and for giving me the chance to take care of my baby. The worship team began playing. I was standing there praying, my eyes closed, and all of the sudden I realize the first song they start with is "It is Well with My Soul," my favorite song, the one I talked about when I prayed while in ICU.

I lost it! I was crying. I was shaky. I was so humbled by God and by my chapel family. I just had to leave. I was too emotional. My husband helped me walk out to the foyer. It was too overwhelming for me with all that happening inside, and the way things happened. Was that a coincidence too? No, it was not!

My God was and is with me always. That night at church was one of the most humble nights I had ever experienced.

I know my purpose is to grow God's kingdom and to love even the unlovable, to reach the unreachable, and, of course, to raise and train my son in all of the ways of the Lord. Proverbs 22:6(NKJV), 1Timothy 4:13(ESV).

My son, Jared, turned 15 years old this year, 2013, and I couldn't be more proud of him. Jared loves church. He goes to the weekend service with his family. He goes to BCY, Believers Chapel Youth, once a week, and he recently joined a life group for teenagers. Jared has a faith in God far beyond his years. He has a passion for sharing God's word and truth with people. He does well academically. He is a great big brother to his sister. Jared and I have a close relationship. I think we can talk about anything. Sure, he's a normal teenager and there may be some things that he might be more comfortable talking about with his dad or a friend, but our time together is precious to me. I'm thankful to be his mother.

Remembering back to one of my regular neurologist visits while in recovery, Tony and I asked many questions. The main question being could I have another baby someday, once I'm fully recovered? They told us no, that it would be too much stress for my body to go through. They said that my body had been through so much and it couldn't handle the stress of delivering another baby. I don't remember if I said it out loud or in my head but I said, "Yeah, right. I'm going to have another baby."

I must admit they were correct in saying that my body was very messed up. I didn't have a menstrual cycle for about a year and then not a normal one for a very long time. I worked diligently to restore my mental, physical, and emotional strength. I prayed regularly that we could have another baby. I believed that God showed me that I would indeed have another child. Though I knew I wasn't near ready, I continued praying about it, totally believing I would be blessed with another child.

Several years went by. On the months I didn't have a period (as my periods were irregular), I thought maybe this would be the month that I was pregnant, but I'd take a pregnancy test and it would be negative. I began to get discouraged. Any of you who is trying to get pregnant know exactly what this disappointment feels like month after month.

I remember feeling very content with our family of three, so I started questioning my feelings. I thought maybe I misunderstood God. I remember thinking how could I have another baby? Will my body even be able to? How could I love another child as much as I love my son? I consciously decided to stop thinking about it and I stopped taking monthly pregnancy tests. I already felt so blessed with our family.

But I truly felt like God showed me (during my recovery) that I would indeed have another baby. Though I was content, I continued to pray for a baby blessing.

Almost seven years later, on February 8, 2005, we welcomed a beautiful healthy baby girl, Jada Lee Tricome, into the world. Pregnancy was definitely harder on my body this time. I was also seven years older. I had terrible sciatic nerve pain and an iron deficiency. I was always tired before I got pregnant, so for me this pregnancy felt extra exhausting. I couldn't take my migraine medications during pregnancy. But my little angel had arrived, weighing 7lbs 15oz, and she was healthy. What more could I ask for? She was born six years and two months before her brother turned 7. We were ecstatic. This precious bundle of joy added so much to our family! She's Mommy's Little Angel. Another miracle from God! Jared was so happy to have a little sister.

There was an effect on my relationships and a strain on my marriage during my sickness and recovery. As I talked about earlier, my heart was hurt, even broken, when I went home to be with my baby, longing to be his mommy—only to find out that he didn't want Mom anymore, he only wanted his grandma. I have to say that I do not blame my mother for this in any way. It's natural for the baby to get attached to the caregiver. My mom is such a blessing to us. She took care of my baby for almost two months, morning, noon, and night. I didn't have to worry about him and Tony didn't have to worry about him because we knew he was in great hands and safe! However, it was still painful to have your baby reach for someone else and squirm away from you and crawl to them. I missed the way it used to be before I got sick. He always wanted his mommy then.

I felt so sad that I had missed his milestones. I missed him getting new teeth and all the new hair he had. He changed so much and was so big. It was amazing all the changes in just two months. All I wanted to do was be with Jared. I wanted to work on him getting to know me again, work on getting him to want me again.

I put everything I had into my relationship with my son. It worked. Over the next 3-5 months, we got close again. I couldn't have been be happier. Or so I thought. I had convinced myself that I was the same person that I was before I got sick; I wanted everyone to see me as they did before. I just wanted to be normal. I was sick of feeling embarrassed all the time. I was sick of people looking at me differently.

We found a new house about six months after I came home from rehab, after looking at nearly 100 houses. We found what we believed to be "the house," the one we felt God showing us that this was the one for us. It was a ranch house. For me this was huge. Though I was walking well and recovering well, stairs were not my friend. Carrying laundry to and from the basement was challenging and now add a one-year-old energetic little boy to that...it was difficult, to say the least. This house needed a lot of work, but it was in foreclosure and it was affordable. We put in an offer on the spot and they accepted it immediately. We were thrilled. At last, a new chapter for us to start.

We got moved in and settled. We loved our new home with no stairs; it was perfect for us. We realized how blessed we were. God worked everything out with the townhouse. We had tenants that rented it the day we moved out. I finally felt like things were moving forward. I was ready to try and leave some things in the past.

I was still working on myself and always improving. It broke my heart to leave Jared even for a few hours to work. I returned to Supercuts, doing about 20 hours at first. I returned with all of my regular responsibilities: office duties, hair cutting and styling. It was awful leaving Jared; we'd just gotten close again. I often wondered if he looked around the house for me and thought, *did mommy abandoned me again?*

Your mind can be a terrible thing. Mine definitely played tricks on me. When I was home, I spent every minute with my baby, but we were definitely going through a financial strain at that time. I kept telling myself everything would be okay, at least we're all together. But I wanted to contribute financially. I remember having to buy Dollar Store deodorant and many of our necessities there. We had our normal bills like everyone, but I also had many new doctor bills. Neither of us had a paycheck for nearly two months. He didn't return to work until I came home.

I bumped up my hours, trying to work up to 30 hours a week to help. I was still working on being healthy and trying to do all that I did before I got sick. Every day was a challenge. Now not only did I struggle with my daily living tasks but also with everyday work tasks. I knew Tony was stressed. I felt bad because I knew it was kind of my fault. All those medical bills…

I worked hard and did my best. I told him I was fine, but I told everyone I was fine. Unfortunately I wasn't fine. I was constantly stressed out at work because I was unable to do my normal tasks. Common tasks like opening the safe were a challenge. Somehow I couldn't do it even with the combination in front of me. I struggled with all the paperwork. It took me so long to add the weekly numbers. For some reason I would add them, get the answer, but then add again a second time to be sure and I'd get a different answer from the first one. There were days I'd add the weekly numbers five or six times and I would get five or six different answers. I was so overwhelmed! I was able to do stuff like cutting and styling with no problem, though I was very uncomfortable talking—doing consultations, greeting clients, and answering the phones were almost painful for me.

No one really knew any of this except God. I was embarrassed to admit that I was struggling so much with such easy things, mortified that my simple tasks were now huge tasks. I really felt like I was now a mentally retarded person. I still didn't like talking much, only when I had to. I went from being a pretty confident person to having no confidence at all. I couldn't remember anything. My brain was in overload everyday all day long.

Tony would tell me something and then later on or a different day talk to me about it again and I'd say, "You're crazy, you didn't tell me that." I really believed he didn't tell me—and if he did, how could my brain not remember it? I used to have an amazing memory and could multitask like nobody's business. This frustration would often be the start of an argument. I wouldn't remember and believe he didn't tell me something and then we'd bicker about it. This often happened with family and friends too, but I would totally downplay it. I don't believe they ever caught on. No one knew how bad I was but Tony.

One day, I realized how distant Tony and I seemed with each other. We would argue over money, or work, or me forgetting things. We didn't have an intimate relationship anymore. I was stressed. We both were stressed. It seemed like nothing was getting any easier.

We had always had an amazing relationship—respectful, fun, and loving—one that most people dreamed of having. I remember praying and asking God what Tony's problem was. I mean, hello! The past year and half had been the hardest of my life, mentally, physically, and emotionally! What was up with him?

I was a basketcase. I was extremely tired since I got sick and suffered from intense migraines almost daily. My neurologist said because I had migraines as a kid, now, with the added trauma to my brain, my headaches would be more frequent and could be more intense. He was correct. I asked all of my doctors why I was always so tired. They would just say it was normal after all the stress my body went through. I figured I just needed to find a way to go on and live a fulfilled life with these new challenges.

I was sad over my marriage. We were still nice to each other and did most things together, but it was far from what we had. I prayed and asked the Lord what happened to Tony. Was it because he didn't find me attractive? Because of how I looked? The top part of my head was shaved and my face was blown up from the steroids, plus I was breaking out with teenage-like acne from all the drugs.

Was it because of how I talked or that I couldn't think clearly, or how I couldn't do many things without help? I remember crying and praying, "Lord, what is it? I feel like I live with my brother. I mean, I love this man dearly, but an occasional peck on the cheek in passing as we worked opposite shifts so one of us could always be with Jared, this definitely was not a romantic relationship." I asked, "Why, God?" Please show Tony what is happening to us."

God heard my prayers and my cry for help. However, to my surprise, God showed me that what had happened between us was not Tony's fault.

It was my doing. I did this to my marriage.

God showed me that I had put my husband on the back burner; I slighted him and pushed him away by putting everything I had into my son. With everything that was going on in my head and my body, now this? "How could this be, Lord?" I asked. I seriously didn't believe I had the strength to fix this! I don't have the energy! I just have too many things to think about. My brain is so overloaded. I felt like a baby that's highly overstimulated; I wanted to just quit and cry and be done with everything. But I continued to pray and think and pray and think.

I knew God did not heal me and bring me this far to quit on my son or to quit on my husband or on my marriage. I knew that this was the man of my dreams. How could this have happened? How did we get from madly in love to this place? I knew what I had to do. So like a dog with its tail between its legs, I approached Tony and said, "Things are different in our marriage. I feel like I'm married to my brother, not to someone I'm in love with romantically. I have to believe that you feel the same way."

I was shocked by his reaction. He was angry and bitter. I told him that I had been praying and asking God to show him what went wrong, but instead God showed me that it wasn't him, it was me. I explained how God showed me that I put Tony on the back burner and how I put Jared before everything else. I apologized and asked him to forgive me. I explained that it wasn't intentional—I didn't even know I was doing it. I was totally unaware of it. Again, I said, "Please forgive me so we can work on having our amazing relationship back."

Well, things were very difficult for a while. I could feel my marriage falling apart. I knew we both loved each other very much, though we didn't act very in love at that time. I knew we both loved God. My husband just couldn't forgive me. He was so hurt and angry. I began to understand his perspective of our relationship, to see his hurt and anger. I mean, this man was at my bedside for nearly two months—praying over me, feeding me, wiping me, clipping my nails—he helped me do everything. And I came home and put everything I had into my baby so he would want his mommy again, completely ignoring the man who helped me through it all. I felt terrible. I did all that I knew to do to express how sorry I was to him, yet he still struggled to forgive me. I thought I would never hurt him on purpose, and I was trying to fix it.

I apologized many times and asked for forgiveness. I definitely was losing my patience over this because I felt we weren't going anywhere. I just wanted to fix it and move on. In one of our heated conversations, I said, "If you truly can't forgive me, then what are we doing? Why would you want to stay with me? Why are we together? Can we even have a real relationship without forgiving? Jesus forgives everyone who asks. We would be living like hypocrites without forgiveness. We go to church every week, we appear to be happy, but we truly aren't. I can't live this way and I know you don't want to either, right?"

Things were rough for a little while, but he did find the grace to forgive me. We were able to repair our marriage with a lot of prayer, patience, and obedience to God. We did a lot of reading and studying. We used many resources. The Bible, different ministries on radio and television like Joyce Meyer, Charles Stanley, and Jimmy Evans all helped. And books from these speakers, and whatever I could find at Sacred Melody Christian bookstore.

I am happy to say that we came back to each other and are still in love and very happy. God showed me that being married truly is a choice. Love is a choice. Even when it's awkward or feels strange to show someone who suddenly feels like a stranger love and affection. God will honor your obedience to that stranger and he can and will restore your relationship. Keep God first. Be obedient to his word and to his prompting. It wasn't long before it stopped feeling awkward or like going through motions. It felt like love again. I was lucky enough to marry to my best friend and I'm more in love with him than when we first fell in love.

With God love is a choice. Matthew 19:26(NLT) "Jesus looked at them intently and said, "Humanly speaking, it is impossible." But with God everything is possible."

The next year and a half we spent working on our family and our finances, with me still trying to sort through all of my own issues from being sick. I was still a senior manager for Supercuts in Syracuse. I loved doing hair and I loved my job before I got sick, but since being sick and having brain damage, my job was nothing but stress. It was all the office duties I struggled with, and I hated being away from Tony and Jared. I attempted to do simple tasks at work, but I was unsuccessful and extremely frustrated. It seemed the more I tried to figure problems out or the more I put into my brain, the harder it was for me to concentrate and the more migraines I had. The more I had to think about something, the worse my speech was. I often locked my office door and just cried and prayed. I wondered if I'd ever be normal again. I tried to act like my old self. I began looking like my old self on the outside, but inside I felt like a hot mess. When people would talk to me, I paid close attention so I understood and replied correctly. I tried so hard to not look ignorant because I didn't understand things. I tried so hard to stay with the conversation. I often forgot midway through what people were talking about. I was frustrated. I knew I had gotten better with this over the past year, but I just wanted to be normal again.

I realized that my job wasn't working and that something had to change. I was tired of being overloaded. My brain felt exhausted; my body was always exhausted. I asked my doctor why I was so tired and he looked at me like I was nuts for complaining. After all I been through, my doctor said I was lucky to be alive. I tried not to complain. Most people didn't even have a clue as to what I was going through or how I felt. I just wanted to know if this was ever going to change or would I always feel this way. I believe my doctor was shocked by my progress. I was very thankful for my progress and for my successes, but it's challenging to be different in every way and still try and do the same tasks.

I prayed everyday about my job and for our family. During my prayer time, I started to feel like God was showing me that I would work from home. Well, the thought of that didn't seem like an option. I prayed and read the Bible to stay strong in my faith. I felt pulled in many directions. It felt like my brain didn't rest. I knew God was the truth and the way and I didn't want to ever lose faith, so I asked the Lord what I was to do. I knew I wouldn't be able to continue my job much longer. I'd done hair since 1990 and I managed people. That's what I did. I didn't know anything else. I was tired of crying and feeling stupid every day. Anyone who knew me knew this wasn't my normal character. I would never just sit and wallow. If there was a problem, I would fix it and move on. I certainly wouldn't cry over it, but this I couldn't fix; no matter how much I willed my brain to work and remember things, it just wasn't working.

I didn't feel normal in anyway. Everything in my life was different. The way I looked, the way I acted, the way I walked, and the way I talked. Every relationship changed. I couldn't pretend any longer. I knew I had to accept that this was the new me. Let me reassure you, I was plenty thankful for my progress. With that said, it was still humiliating as I struggled to cope with the new me. Even some of my employees said things like "you seem so different," or "you're soft now since you got sick." The truth was I didn't have the energy to correct and enforce things at work.

At the same time, many of my employees shared that they'd begun praying and leaning on God and getting to know him better as a result of all that happened to me. Well, I was thrilled to hear that. I had shared things about God for years with some of them, but many times I felt my sharing fell on deaf ears. God definitely was using my sickness to open people's eyes.

During my prayer time, God was still showing me that I was going to work from home. I knew I had to share this idea with Tony. I was reluctant because I knew it was such an impossibility, but I told him. I shared what God had been showing me. He basically said I was dreaming, and that it's a nice dream, and he wished it could be true, but it's impossible—he dismissed it. He didn't share in my enthusiasm. After some time passed, I brought it up to him again. This time it was crystal clear to me. I knew that I was going to work from home. I shared some of the things I had been struggling with at work, and how I wasn't the same person prior to being sick. I explained how hard it was for me to admit all of this, and that I didn't mean to deceive him or anyone, I just wanted desperately to be my old self again. I said that I couldn't do my job well and I didn't think I could do my job much longer, and that I believed the Lord showed me that I was going to work from home. I could sense his aggravation with me. I knew full well that we had so much debt and so many bills, mostly because of me, and now I was telling him that I couldn't do my job…

I let him ponder the idea for a while and gave him some space, but he still said it was an impossibility. Well, when God shows you something, it doesn't just go away. In fact, it got stronger and stronger. I knew it would happen. Honestly, I didn't even think or consider *how* it would happen. I just believed God. I kept my eyes on him, not on the mountain that was in front of me.

Meanwhile, at work, my boss told me that the manager convention was coming up. This was a mandatory conference held once a year out of state. I remember looking at my boss, sitting in my office, and saying, "Honestly, I'm appalled that you would even think that I would leave my family right now after everything I've been through. I'm not going anywhere!"

My boss showed some compassion and kind of understood. But his boss, not so much. He relayed back to me that if I wanted to keep my senior manager position, I would be on that trip.

I then said, without hesitation, "I'm no longer your senior manager!"

My boss told me to think about it and to talk it over with Tony. He said not to make a hasty decision, but I assured him that he'd heard my decision—I wasn't the senior manager anymore. Then I went into the bathroom and cried and prayed, realizing what I'd just done.

I called Tony to tell him the news. My voice was shaky but I explained what took place and what I said. At first, I got complete silence on the phone. I think he was in shock. He asked if I would get a pay cut, and I knew I would, so I said yes, but I didn't know how much less. He did understand why I wouldn't go on that trip after all that our family had been through. I was relieved that he didn't expect me to go. He said we would be all right. I could hear the disappointment in his voice, and the fear, as we barely made it with my current salary.

I continued praying, and got the same word every time, that I was going to work from home. For a moment, I looked at this idea through human eyes. *Tony was right! It's just not possible,* I thought. All I could do from home was maybe babysit. I brought it up to Tony again. I told him how positive I was of this. I suggested me being a babysitter. He said I was crazy, that I could never do daycare in our home. He was right. Shortly after my recovery, I showed signs of Obsessive-Compulsive Disorder. If another kid put my son's toys in his mouth, or even just played with them, I would disinfect them as soon as the kid left. I was a little nuts for a short time after I was sick. My doctors told me that I got sick from a germ, that I went through all of this because of a germ, and well, I wasn't going to let my baby get sick like I did from a germ! Like I said, I went a little nuts. A little out there. I'd like to add that God worked out my OCD. I'm not nearly extreme as I was then. I'm just germ conscientious now.

Tony had another good point. I couldn't babysit all day with my migraines and always feeling tired and overwhelmed, either. That wouldn't be smart or responsible. But there had to be something I could do from home.

It wasn't long after this that I realized what God was showing me was that I would be doing hair from home. The problem with that was we had no money and no space to do it in. Our driveway was dirt and stone, and our house had siding, but kind of an ugly red/brown color—it wasn't professional at all. I thought, *okay, God, I know this is going to happen.* I was so sure. I told Tony, who laughed at me and said it would never happen. It was strange—I didn't get mad at all. I simply believed it would and no one could tell me different.

I began telling other people. I told my mom and she said, "Bren, Tony said that's not going to happen."

I told friends and they said, "No, Bren, Tony says no," or "that's a nice dream, maybe someday."

And I'd smile and say, "Oh, it's for real and it's going to be soon."

Everyone knew that Tony did all of our bills and took care of all of our finances as I was unable to do any of it since my sickness. In fact, part of my rehab was learning to write checks, etc. That's why everyone said, "No, Bren, Tony said no." They knew I wouldn't be able to start anything without his approval.

Now I was getting under Tony's skin. He told me to stop telling people that this was going to happen. We went back and forth, neither of us bending. I remember I felt so sure and had such a peace about this, like when I saw the angels and heard the music. I knew it would work out, even though on paper it was impossible. Nothing was on our side and that was what Tony was looking at. He was looking at the facts, what our bills were and how much income we had and how much something like this would cost. It was impossible on paper!

I asked him to pray about it and he said, "Why? There is nothing to pray about, these are the facts."

I asked him again to pray about it. Well, he reluctantly prayed about it, and soon after, maybe a week or two later, he was completely on board with the idea! We asked a contractor friend to help us come up with a blueprint to add on to our house. He agreed and also signed on to do the project. I'm still not sure how we got this done, but we re-sided our house, removed some trees, and paved the stone driveway. We had a garage built with extra space behind it to turn into the salon, and the salon had its own entrance/walkway to so it was completely separate from our home.

My husband and a few others repeatedly asked if I really thought that people would come to my house for a haircut. All I knew was that God said I would do hair from home. I never asked how, I just said, "Okay, God, let's do it!"

Brenda's Hair Design opened in November 2001. Another miracle from God. I advertised in several local papers and already had many clients follow me that had been following me from salon to salon for years.

Another amazing thing happened. I received a call for an appointment from a new client who saw my advertisement. She said her parents were visiting her from China and she saw my ad and wanted to make an appointment for her mother to get her hair colored and her dad to get a haircut. She said her parents spoke no English and she would come to interpret. I said great and made the appointments. They showed up as scheduled. Right away I thought this lady looked familiar. I introduced myself and draped her mother and started applying her hair color, then I asked her to have a seat and offered her a magazine. Her daughter told her what I said and got her settled while I draped the dad and communicated with the daughter about what kind of haircut he wanted. I did the cut & he seemed very satisfied.

Her mom still had about 15 or 20 minutes to sit and let her color process, so I took a few moments to relax and make conversation. As I sat in my chair, I couldn't help but stare at this lady. She was Chinese with black hair cut into a short bob. She looked to be nine months pregnant. I knew that I knew her, but I couldn't place from where. She noticed me staring at her and I finally said, "You look very familiar."

She said, "No, no, I don't think so."

"I'm sure of it," I said.

She said "no" again, but I was sure of it.

I said, "I'm positive I know you from somewhere." I thought, *geez, I may forget most things but I never forget a face.*

"Where do you work?"

"I don't work right now," she said, and pointed down to her pregnant belly. She said she was out of work on maternity leave.

"Where did you work?" I asked again.

"I'm a doctor."

I knew it! That was it! She took care of me! "You're a doctor at Crouse Hospital, right?" She seemed puzzled, so I continued. "You took care of me when I was in Crouse. Every morning, you shined a light in my eyes and asked me if I knew where I was. 'You know your name? Can you raise your arm and point to your nose?' Of course I couldn't do it back then," I said.

She got excited then. "Refresh my memory," she said, "and tell me what you had."

When I said I had meningitis that went to the brain and caused cerebellitis, she jumped to her feet and said, "You in corner bed in intensive care! I remember! Oh my God! You walk! You work! We think you no walk again." She was shocked. I think she even hugged my arm for a second.

It was amazing! I knew that Brenda's Hair Design was a God thing! I praised God for that confirmation. I have been open for 11 years now. God has used my business to (besides making people look beautiful) share and minister to people. I have had many opportunities to pray with clients and invite them to church. Many have visited my church and some come regularly. I never push God on anyone. I think my clients can testify to that. It's a personal decision that everyone must make on their own. Besides, God is a gentleman and won't push himself on anyone. He simply extends an invitation. I'm thankful that I get to do what I love to do and plant many seeds along the way.

Part Three:
Life Today

Today my life is amazing. It's hard for me to believe that 14 years have gone by. I have the most amazing husband and two fabulous children. I'm a successful salon owner. I have accepted myself for who I am and with all of my differences. I do have some daily struggles. I still have short term memory loss, though it has greatly improved over the years. I have migraines almost daily. I have tendonitis in my hands, shoulders, elbows, and I always feel tired. I still get a little confused and struggle to concentrate.

I certainly have learned how to laugh at myself. Most of my challenges go unnoticed by other people, but to me, they are a reminder of all that God has brought me through. I would say my issues are mild. I know that lots of people have hurts and pains daily. It's unfortunately part of life, and we just have to keep pushing through it.

James 1:12-15(NLT) "God blesses the people who patiently endure testing. Afterward they will receive the crown of life that God has promised to those who love him. And remember, no one who wants to do wrong should ever say, "God is tempting me." God is never tempted to do wrong, and he never tempts anyone else. Temptations comes from our own desires. These evil desires lead to evil actions, and evil actions lead to death."

There are days when I'm down with a migraine and can't do much, but I get back up again the next day. One of my favorite sayings is if you have a pulse, then it's a good day. I try to find a blessing in every day, there's always something to be grateful for.

God's presence is all around us. I look at all of the good in my life and it keeps me getting back up. I choose to look at God and not the mountain. On days when I can't remember the simplest things or can't speak correctly, I just think, *wow*, and laugh it off. Some things are just out of our control. My strength truly comes from the Lord. Isaiah 40:28(ESV) Have you not known? Have you not heard? The Lord is the everlasting God, the creator of the ends of the earth, He does not faint or grow weary; his understanding is unsearchable."

I read my Bible daily, usually in the morning, then I'm armed and ready to face this hard and sometimes cruel world. Ephesians 6:11-13(NLT) Put on all of God's armor so that you will be able to stand firm against all strategies and tricks of the devil. For we are not fighting against people made of flesh and blood, but against the evil rulers and authorities of the unseen world, against those mighty powers of darkness who rule this world, and against wicked spirits in the heavenly realms. Use every piece of God's armor to resist the enemy in the time of evil, so that after the battle you will still be standing firm."

I work hard to stay focused on God, my family, and my personal goals. In recent years, I added some new challenges to my life. I signed up for some 5k races, which meant I had to learn how to run and train for them. In addition, I completed two Iron Girl triathlons in 2011 and 2012. Some say it was crazy to have such lofty goals given my medical history, but when my husband said, "Are you crazy? You can't do that!" I was determined. I had to prove him wrong and prove to myself that with proper training and dedication these goals could be reached. I ran three to four miles four or five days a week. I swam 20 laps twice a week at a local pool. I did strength training using weights and the program P90X. I trained hard and pushed myself every day for eight months to train for these races. Some days I couldn't train because of a terrible migraine or because I was simply too tired. I'd train even harder the following day if I missed a day. I confess it was tough training with a headache every day. I had to stop some of my strength training due to my tendonitis. I realized my being able to work was more important than that part of my training so I stopped. My training was long and grueling, but God gave me the strength and the grace to compete.

Philippians 4:13(NLT) For I can do everything through Christ, who gives me the strength I need."

I will not let anyone tell me that I can't do something when God says I can do all things through him who gives me strength. In 2012, I also did a Warrior Run, a 5k up Labrador Mountain. Running up the mountain was the hard part. The obstacles were pure fun.

I know that I am a woman of substance, healed by the grace of God. I'm devoted to growing God's kingdom. I fully understand that there is life after death. I share my story not because I'm special, but because I'm ordinary. God uses ordinary people every day. I'm grateful that I never had to walk this journey alone. I have God by my side, my wonderful husband and family, and some amazing friends. I've learned that no matter who you are, or what you do for a living, or how old you are, you too have a journey. God did not intend for us to go through life on our own. Isaiah 46:4(NLT) "I will be your God throughout your lifetime- until your hair is white with age. I made you, and I will care for you. I will carry you along and save you." I know that I will face more challenges and struggles in the next chapter of my life, but I also know God will be with me.

Everyone should know and understand what your purpose is. Who created you? Why were you created? Matthew 7:7(NIV) Ask and it will be given to you; seek and you will find; Knock and the door will be opened to you." I believe that every one of us is born with a desire to know God. It may be buried deep down, but it's there. Pray and ask God and he will show you what your purpose is. Choose to live your life on purpose.

Engage in a relationship with God, not just a religion. Ask Jesus to live in your heart, and to forgive your sins. Surrender to his ways, his truth. He wants a relationship with you. John 3:16(NIV) "For God so loved the world that he gave his one and only son, that whoever believes in him shall not perish but have eternal life".. People often ask me, how do you have a relationship with God? Think of it this way—what do a boy and girl do when they are in love? They learn about each other, they talk to each other for hours at a time, they ask questions to get to know each other, about likes/dislikes, that kind of stuff, right? Basically, they spend time together getting to know each other. That is what God wants. Pray, read the Bible, talk to him ask him to help you understand, listen to worship music, praise him, find a Bible teaching church. I promise you if you try it, you will completely understand.

The first step is asking Jesus in your heart. John 14:6(NIV) "Jesus answered, I am the way the truth and the life. No one comes to the father except through me." It's not about being a good person, or cleaning up your life and then asking him into your heart. First we must pray and invite him in and then let him work on cleaning up our messy stuff. He becomes our example to follow. He gifts the Bible to us. The Bible has never been disproved. Once you begin to read it, you will quickly realize that it is our instruction book for life. God giving it to us proves of his desire to have a relationship with us.

Have the right perspective. Look at life through

God's eyes. Because we live in a fallen, cursed world and an imperfect world as a result of what happened in the story of Adam and Eve, every single one of us will have to face trials and tribulations as we go through life. When we have a godly perspective, we understand that we will have these trials and tribulations, and we know that God will carry us through them.

We will never understand God's ways completely until we are with him in paradise, but we have faith in him because he is the creator of the world. He is in control. He didn't cause me to get sick. Romans 8:28(NIV) "And wee know that in all things God works for the good of those who love him, who have been called to his purpose." I don't know why I got sick and went through all that I did. I don't know why some people go through even worse things than what I went through. I know God was with me and carried me through it. I know that because of my sickness, many people witnessed God's miracles. I know that as a result, many people formed a relationship with him. We may not see the big picture or the end results, but God knows the end results. God is not the one causing our pain.

1 Peter 5:8 (NIV) "Be self-controlled and alert. Your enemy the devil prowls around like a roaring lion, looking

for someone to devour." Satan is a fallen angel who rebelled against God. He is real, not symbolic, and he is constantly working against God and those who obey him. He tries to hurt us. He tries to get us to blame God for his doings. We may not see the whole plan of God, yet we must trust in his plan.

Something to think about: if every human being accepted Jesus in their heart and followed the Bible, there would be no sin, no murder, no lies, no stealing, no bullying, no adultery, no addictions, no cheating, and no terrorists. We would live in a perfect, peaceful, loving world, the way God designed it to be. God is the creator of the world.

Because of Adam and Eve, we are born into sin. God gave them free will just as he does you and me. The world we live in today is the result of choosing sin. We all have free will, and we can choose to accept God and his full design of the world or not. But we have to make that choice for ourselves. Doing nothing is also a choice. Everything is God's for his purpose. This is our temporary home. We all get attached to things in this world, obviously our family, our children etc. I would be hurt, crushed, devastated if something happened to any of the people I love so much, but I know that my children are a gift from God, they are his first. I'm blessed that he entrusts them to me and I will do my best to care for them and protect them, but ultimately, I know they are only mine temporarily. If my salon started to fail, I would be sad for sure, but I know God will provide for me. If something happened to my home, I would be sick over it. Realizing that everything is God's and not your own keeps life in the right perspective.

True joy and peace comes from the Lord (Isaiah 26:3(KJV) There is a sense of peace and joy that is recognized in a true believer. Sometimes looking at their life or situation might make you want to scream or cry, but when you look at them, they have a calmness, a peacefulness about them. They even have joy. You may wonder what is wrong with them. How can they be so calm when it appears their life is upside down or in shambles? Because they know that God is in control. They know that their life is not their own. All we can do is walk in God's truth. Be obedient to his word. You can't praise God one day because life is going as you planned, but then curse God the next day because your plan is broken. That's not faith. That's a relationship with yourself. That's you trying to control life. God wants us to fully trust and rely on him no matter what.

Please understand that we are all human. We all have moments of frustration, anger, pain, etc. I can only speak for myself. I know my body. I know that after a long day of work or a night of no sleep that my tongue is not going to work right. It just stops working and I can't speak well. I know that my memory is worse at these times, and it is frustrating for me and my family.

There are many times when I feel so alone in a room full of people because not one of them understands what I'm going through or what I'm feeling. How could they possibly understand brain damage? You look good/normal on the outside, but inside you're a hot mess and no one knows it. It's a lonely place to be. I fully rely on God to carry me through these moments. God wants to carry us. He wants the best for us. Regardless of my life's disappointments or hurts, I know this home is temporary.

Praise God during your storms. Not because you are enjoying the storm; praise him because he is God. He is a loving God that hurts when you hurt and sees every tear you cry and he is the only one in control. No one could ever love you more. I know I have a home in heaven for eternity. We all have hurts that no one knows about or understands, but God does. He sees our pain and he is there for us if we'll let him be. Don't be distracted by things that won't matter to your destiny.

When I was in the rehabilitation center, a therapist asked me a very common question. She asked, "What does it mean to say the grass is greener on the other side?" Well, I thought for a few moments— of course I know this. I'd heard it and said it dozens of times. I thought...and thought...at that time, I wasn't able to put it into words for her. I've thought about this for 14 years. It means not to envy what you don't have, but to appreciate what you do have. It's easy to look at others and think they have it all together or think things are perfect for him/her, or that they always get what they want. But before you judge, remember that every human being has trials, burdens, and hardships. They have things going on inside that no one knows about.

Working with the public for many years, I come across every type of person out there. I have to say that I have the best clients in the world, most of them I even call friends. One client has said to me on more than one occasion that they wanted to start going to church with me, so they can have a perfect life like mine. Well, I don't get easily offended, but I certainly was feeling something after that remark. I paused and said, ."Walking into a building doesn't make your life perfect. My life is far from perfect." I know that I'm blessed beyond measure. I also work extremely hard for what I have I know that if I didn't continue to read God's word daily and pray, I would probably have lost faith and given up long ago. But walking into a building changes nothing.

Faith and actions together is what changes circumstances (James 2:14-26(ESV)

I was put off by that statement. It felt like my journey, my testimony was somehow being minimized. It seemed a bit judgmental. I'm sure it was not intended to be. However, we need to be conscious of our words.

Part Four:
Supplement Material

I promised God I'd train my son in all his ways!
This beautiful face reminded me of my promise to God and was my
motivation to push on and never stop!

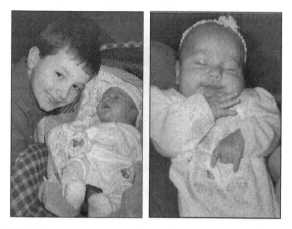

Feb. 8 2005: My little angel was born—(Jada Tricome).

This was the picture on our living room wall that my mom pointed to and said "Momma" several times a day with Jared. After almost two months of not seeing me, he came to visit me in rehab, pointed to me, and said, "Momma."

Brenda's Hair Design has been open now for 11 years.
I am blessed to be able to do what I love to do. I am thankful to
God and all my faithful clients.

This is a picture of me after finishing my first Iron Girl triathlon. I
am a person who has tremendous faith in my God and myself. This
was a great accomplishment.

Here I competed in the Warrior Run race at Labrador Mountain. This race was up a large mountain and had obstacles in water and mud. After all I had been through and my daily challenges, determination was a must to get through these races. When life brings trials and challenges, we must have determination to get through them… I trained my body and mind to make it strong to be able to finish. I exercise my faith daily getting built up by God's word and listening to ministries.

I enjoyed running the swamp rat race with my daughter. She ran 1 mile without stopping. I was so proud of her.

I was so thankful to have four hours
with my family on Christmas Day.

                           DISCHARGE SUMMARY

PATIENT NAME:TRICOME, BRENDA
MEDICAL RECORD NUMBER:0226-254
ACCOUNT NUMBER: 70702741
DATE OF ADMISSION: 12/23/1998
DATE OF DISCHARGE: 12/30/1998
ATTENDING PHYSICIAN: ROBERT J WEBER, MD

DATE OF BIRTH:

ADMISSION DIAGNOSIS: CEREBELLITIS.

DISCHARGE DIAGNOSIS:
1.   CEREBELLITIS.
2.   COGNITIVE DEFICITS.
3.   STACCATIC SPEECH.

HISTORY OF PRESENT ILLNESS: THIS IS A 26-YEAR-OLD WHITE FEMALE WHO WAS IN
HER USUAL STATE OF HEALTH UNTIL MID-NOVEMBER WHEN SHE STARTED DEVELOPING A
FLU-LIKE ILLNESS WHICH PROGRESSED UP UNTIL HER PRESENTATION AT HER PHP
PHYSICIAN WHERE SHE WAS NOTED TO HAVE SOME CEREBELLAR DEFICITS. SHE WAS
ADMITTED TO CROUSE HOSPITAL, AND WORKUP WITH AN MRI SHOWED
CEREBELLITIS-TYPE POSTERIOR FOSSA WITH FOURTH VENTRICLE CONSTRICTION AND
FORWARD DISPLACEMENT OF THE BRAIN STEM. PLEASE SEE THEIR DISCHARGE SUMMARY
FOR HER HOSPITAL COURSE WHILE IN CROUSE HOSPITAL. SHE REMAINED
HEMODYNAMICALLY STABLE DURING THAT ENTIRE STAY. SHE WAS DISCHARGED TO 2
NORTH REHAB ON DECEMBER 23, 1998.

PAST MEDICAL HISTORY: SIGNIFICANT PAST MEDICAL HISTORY OF FOOT INJURY AT 7
YEARS OLD. STATUS POST DEBRIDEMENT.

PAST SURGICAL HISTORY: DEBRIDEMENT OF HER LEFT FOOT.

OBSTETRICAL HISTORY: SHE IS GRAVIDA 1, PARA 1, 0-0-1.

ALLERGIES: SULFA.

MEDICINES ON ADMISSION: ACYCLOVIR 700 MG IV SOLUSET Q.8H., WHICH WAS
CONTINUED UNTIL DECEMBER 28; DECADRON TAPER AS PER DR. AZIZ; ZANTAC;
HEPARIN SUBCU B.I.D.; COLACE.

PHYSICAL EXAMINATION ON ADMISSION: ALERT AND ORIENTED TIMES THREE, IN NO
ACUTE DISTRESS, PLEASANT WITH A FLAT AFFECT, STACCATO SPEECH, TEARFUL, ABLE
TO ANSWER QUESTIONS APPROPRIATELY AND TO STAY ON THE TOPIC. HEENT: NO
NYSTAGMUS. EOMI. PERRLA. CRANIAL NERVES II THROUGH XII GROSSLY INTACT.
HEART: S1 AND S2. REGULAR RATE AND RHYTHM. NO MURMURS DETECTED. LUNGS;
CLEAR TO AUSCULTATION BILATERALLY. ABDOMEN: SOFT AND NONTENDER. POSITIVE
BOWEL SOUNDS. EXTREMITIES: FULL ACTIVE AND PASSIVE RANGE OF MOTION
BILATERAL UPPER AND LOWER EXTREMITIES. NO CLUBBING, CYANOSIS, OR EDEMA.
NO CONTRACTURES. NEUROLOGICAL: SENSATION AND MOTOR WERE INTACT IN
BILATERAL UPPER AND LOWER EXTREMITIES. NO ABNORMAL TONE. HER GAIT SHOWED

TRICOME ,BRENDA L   MR#: 226254   BDATE: SEX: F RACE: W
                                      14:43 04/26/13 From HB1G SMPRTGF1
06/10/2009 @13:45

Living life believing God's word
vs
Living life on how I feel

The most important thing I learned on this journey was about being in control of my life, my thoughts and my choices. Sometimes we make permanent decisions based on how we feel. Sometimes our feelings get the best of us. We rely on how we feel to dictate our life. On many occasions I felt inadequate, lonely, dumb, different, and frustrated. I had anxiety over what I thought other people would think of me, how I looked, how I talked etc., but the bible taught me that God said I can do all things through Christ. God gives us the strength that we don't have. I learned what the Bible says that I am, what God thinks about me and can compare it to what I feel about myself. Jeremiah 1:5(ESV) "Before I formed you in the womb I knew you, and before you were born I consecrated you." Psalm 139:14(ESV) "I am fearfully and wonderfully made." Matthew 10:30(ESV) "The hairs on your head are numbered." Psalm 17:8(ESV) "Keep me as the apple of your eye; hide me in the shadow of your wings." John 3:16(NIV) God gave his only son to die on a cross in my place. Once I learned what God thought about me through these and many other verses, I had to choose to believe the Bible (God's word), which has never changed, or believe my feelings.

Unfortunately, my feelings changed daily. Though I recognized and praised God for my recovery and my life, I was still overwhelmed with feelings of frustration & worthlessness for being so different from how I used to be. I still felt angry, sad, and lonely. The worst for me was feeling defeated. Our brain is a funny thing; it's always taking in information. The enemy likes to confuse us with our feelings.

Through all the scriptures I studied, God showed me that I needed to rewire my brain and change my thought process. If God created me in his image & through his word, I know he is a loving, gracious, caring God.

Then how could I possibly believe that I'm worthless or defeated? How could I be the apple of his eye if I feel awful and continue to express all of these negative emotions that I was feeling daily?

Sometimes when we suffer through trials and life-changing events, we start to feel unloved, or that God is mad at us. We've all been there. But the scriptures say differently. Satan lies to us, he wants us to believe we are worthless and nothing to God. He wants us to blame God for everything bad that happens to us. 1Peter 5:8(NLT) "Be careful! Watch out for attacks from the Devil, your great enemy. He prowls around like a roaring lion, looking for some victim to devour." John 10:10(NIV) "The thief's purpose is to steal and kill and destroy. My purpose is to give life in all its fullness."

I have learned to trust the Bible, and every word in it. The Bible was written years ago, yes, by men, but inspired by God! There was a time when I thought, *can I really trust the Bible knowing it's written by men?* After studying it and praying for God's help to understand what I was reading, I learned the content in it—it's obvious it could in no way be written by man alone. It was written thousands years ago and predicted things in current news. It's impossible.

The Bible has never been disproven. The word of God is alive. When you read it and seek to understand it you will find meaning and guidance for your exact situation. You can read the same verse of scripture years later and have a whole new understanding for your current situation; the scripture didn't change, but it comes alive with our daily life/ trials.

God loves us so much that he gives us this book to help us through every struggle, every trial. The Bible is not just a book of what to do or not to do. God gives it to us to instruct & protect us. If we choose not to follow it, how than can we say it's not true, or it's just a bunch of rules? That's the furthest from the truth. It's designed for us to seek God's truth to read daily for instruction. God's rules are only to protect us and to keep us safe. We shouldn't start reading the Bible only when we have a major storm or when we hit rock bottom and have nowhere else to turn. God wants to have a relationship with us now. He wants us to recognize his love for us. He has never turned his back on us; we are the ones who turn our backs on him.

The closer I get to God the more I understand his ways. Proverbs 3:5(NIV) "Trust in The Lord with all your heart and lean not on your own understanding." Today I choose my words carefully based on who God says I am. The temptation is always there. Even as I'm writing these words the devil is trying to give me ungodly thoughts and feelings—you're not a writer, you're incapable of writing, no one will read this, who are you to write a book, you're not smart, you can't even spell. Thank God for spell check. I honestly can feel the darts he is throwing at me. However, I'm choosing to believe God and his word.

No more of the devil's lies. Ephesians 6:10-17(NIV) talks about putting on the armor of God so that we can stand against the devils schemes. Philippians 4:8(NIV) says to think whatever is noble, right, pure and lovely. The next time you talk negative to yourself remember what God says about you.

Remember how much he loves you. Also remember the devil is the true liar and he will do anything to separate you from God. Ephesians 6:12(NIV) "For our struggle is not against flesh and blood, but against the rulers, against the authorities, against the powers of this dark world and against the spiritual forces of evil in the heavenly realms". We are in a spiritual battle: God vs. the devil. 2 Chronicles 20:17(NIV) God has already won this fight! We too have a part to play as we are in a relationship together. Our part is trusting God and believing his word, reading the Bible daily, and choosing to live according to God's rules vs. man's rules, praying and always seeking God.

Make the choice to believe and trust God today. Let's not stroll through life up and down based on how you feel at any particular moment! Our true joy comes from The Lord. Joy is not based on our circumstances. Nehemiah

8:10(ESV) The joy of the Lord is our strength

These same verses of scripture apply to what we think about others and how we see other people. We all have those friends, family members, coworkers, and acquaintances that we just can't stand sometimes. For some of us, it may be most of the time. It's easy to say, "Love them like Jesus," but, in all honesty, we all struggle with liking them, much less loving them (I know I have). John 13:34-35 (ESV) "A new command I give you, love one another as I have loved you, so you must love one another." 1 Peter 4:8(ESV) "Above all keep loving one another earnestly, since love covers a multitude of sins." Colossians 3:12 -15 (ESV) "Put on then as God's chosen ones, holy and beloved, compassionate hearts, kindness, humility, meekness, and patience bearing with one another and if one has a complaint against another; forgiving as The Lord has forgiven you, so you must also forgive. And above all these put on love, which binds everything together in perfect harmony." Matthew 5:44 (ESV) "But I say to you, Love your enemies pray for those who persecute you" 1Corinthians13:13 (ESV) So now faith, hope and love abide, these three; but the greatest of these is love.

Once we know God and understand his character it's

easier to imitate God. John 13:15(ESV) "For I have given you an example, so that you can do just as I have done to you" Hebrew 13:1(ESV) "Let brotherly love continue" We must choose to forgive each other, to love each other. It's a choice we consciously have to make daily.

It's easy to love lovely kind of people, the ones who are joyful and fun. Luke 6:32(NIV) "If you love those who love you, what benefit is it to you; for even sinners Love those who love them." Luke 6:27-36(NIV) "But I tell you who hear me: Love your enemies, Do good to those who hate you." 2 Timothy2:23-26(NIV) "Don't have anything to do with foolish, stupid arguments, because you know they produce quarrels. And The Lord's servant must not quarrel; instead, he must be kind to everyone, able to teach, not resentful." The majority of our arguments/quarrels/disagreements are usually over issues that do not affect our salvation, our eternal home. Usually it's over hurt feelings or feeling offended. We allow our feelings to determine our actions rather than following what the biblical teachings are. Once we grasp the idea of rewiring our brain and believing and trusting and following the word of God, we can truly love the way God intended us to love each other.

We begin to look at each other through God's eyes.

We are mindful of our thoughts and reactions. We realize we have self-control. And understand how much love God has for all people equally as he does for us. That principle makes it difficult to be harsh and unloving to even the people who seem to be unlikable or unloving. Yes, even the ones that hurt us repeatedly. How can we tell the creator that he made someone wrong just because our personalities clash or someone gets on our nerves? There will always be people who make poor choices, lie, and do things we feel is wrong. We must accept the fact that God is God and he will judge accordingly in his time. Sometimes it seems we want to be a part of or witness their judgment; it's like we don't want them to get away with anything. My friend God does not miss a thing! We were not created to be judge and jury for others. Let's focus on ourselves and what God's plan is for our lives.

Every day choosing to be his light in this very dark world, let's spread love. Every day is a new opportunity to show God's love and grace to people, some who don't deserve it, but every one of us are sinners and are deserving of punishment. Jesus took it all for us John 3:16(NIV). The least we can do is follow his example.

We can only control ourselves. One day we will all stand before the Lord for our actions and every word that comes out of our mouth. We must not let someone else's ugliness or sourness change our character or let them have control of us. God gives us the tools we need to do what he requires us to do and that's to love one another unconditionally. There should never be conditions on love. However, there may be certain circumstances that call for specific boundaries to protect yourself in abusive relationships. I recommend you seek council from you church leadership/pastors in these specific instances.

There are many resources available for us, no matter what your circumstances are. But remember we are responsible for doing the work.

I challenge you to find out what your purpose is in life, if you don't know it.

Choose to live your life on purpose.

There is a book for every situation and circumstance in your life, for whatever difficulty you are going through. There is material to guide you, encourage you, and motivate you. My first choice is the Bible; it is our instruction book for life. A great place to start is 1John 5(NIV).

Music has been a part of my life since I was a kid. It encourages, inspires, and motivates me. My favorite is Christian music artist Third Day, also Casting Crowns, Toby Mac, Lincoln Brewster, Chris Tomlin, Hill song and K-love radio station.

I pray that you will seek to grow your relationship with God.

I pray that this book will bless you and inspire you as you journey through this life. And that you never lose faith or hope. Let God help you to get back up again. Fully rely on God. It's unfortunate the number of people that cross my path weekly that feel helpless, depressed, some ready to give up...

With God, all things are possible. God desires to know you.

Perseverance is a great virtue to have. The Bible has some great encouraging words on the importance of persevering through trials and tribulation. I pray that one of these scriptures or quotes speaks to you.

"Perseverance is not a long race, it's many short races one after another"~ Walter Elliott

Galatians 6:9(NIV) "Let us not become weary in doing good, for at the proper time will reap a harvest if we do not give up."

"Saints are sinners who kept on going"
~ Robert Stevenson

Revelation 3:11(NIV)"I am coming soon. Hold fast what you have, so that no one may seize your crown."

"Problems are not stop signs, they are guidelines"
~ Robert Schuller

Proverbs 3:5-6(NIV) Trust in the Lord with all your heart, and do not lean on your own understanding. In all your ways acknowledge him, and he will make strong your paths."

"I may not be there yet but I'm closer than I was yesterday." ~ Unknown

"With ordinary talent and extra ordinary perseverance, all things are attainable"~ Thomas Foxwell Buxton

"When your dreams turn to dust, vacuum"~ Unknown

"Most people never run far enough on their first wind to find out they've got a second wind"~ William James

"Never think God's delays are God's denials. Hold on: hold fast: hold out. Patience is genius"
~ George Louis Leclerc

Acknowledgments

Thanks to my Lord Jesus Christ for your faithfulness and unfailing love.

Many thanks to my husband, Tony Tricome, for countless hours of advice, help, and encouragement. He was the first to read and edit this book. He offered insight, and suggestions. He stood by me every step of the way throughout my sickness and throughout our relationship. I am blessed to be married to such a loving, helpful man.

Thanks to my son, Jared, for motivating me even when you were just a baby, knowing you were home pushed me to work harder so I could come home and take care of you. And now that you are 15, you motivate me to share my story and to share all that the Lord has done for me and our family.

Thanks to my sweet daughter, Jada, for constantly reminding me of the simple things in life, reminding me to slow down and smell the roses.

Thanks to my mother, Kitty Elkins, for your selfless love, for taking care of my baby when I was sick, and forgiving up your life to move in with us so that I could come home.

Thanks to our family and friends for your countless prayers and acts of kindness over the years.

Thanks to the late Paul Wagner and Believers Chapel for being there for me and my family during such a difficult time.

Thanks to everyone who prayed for me and for my family. Prayer works.

About the Author

Brenda Tricome has been a Christian for 20 years. She has dedicated herself to Christianity and Family. She has a love for people. A deep concern for the hurting and broken - hearted, and a true desire to help them find true joy, and Godly peace. Brenda and her husband Tony have two children and resides in Cicero, N.Y.

Connect with Brenda Tricome

mailto:bltbeep@twcny.rr.com

https://www.facebook.com/BrendaTricome

Twitter: @brenjjto

Made in the USA
Charleston, SC
24 May 2014